The Word of the Prophets of God Is Being Fulfilled
From Abraham to Gabriele

The Word of the Prophets of God
Is Being Fulfilled

FROM
ABRAHAM
TO
GABRIELE

THE WORD
THE UNIVERSAL SPIRIT

The Word of the Prophets of God Is Being Fulfilled
From Abraham to Gabriele

First Edition, March 2014

Published by:
© Universal Life - The Inner Religion
PO Box 3549, Woodbridge, CT 06525
USA

Licensed edition
Translated from the original German title:
Das Wort der Propheten erfüllt sich
von Abraham bis Gabriele
Order No. S 465en

From the Universal Life Series
with the consent of
© Gabriele-Verlag Das Wort
Max-Braun-Str. 2
97828 Marktheidenfeld/Altfeld, Germany

ISBN 978-1-890841-63-8

*For as the rain and the
snow come down from heaven
and do not return there
but water the earth,
making it bring forth and sprout,
giving seed to the sower
and bread to the eater,
so shall my word be
that goes out from my mouth;
it shall not return to me empty,
but it shall accomplish that which I purpose,
and shall succeed in the thing
for which I sent it.*

(Isaiah 55:10-11)

Table of Contents

Foreword

The works of the prophets of God throughout all the centuries ultimately form the basis for the cultural history of mankind; now as before, the major religions refer to the word of the Eternal One through the prophets. And yet today, the emissaries of God, particularly in so-called Christianity, are disparaged as merely a kind of ancestral gallery from long ago.

The cult priesthood, which the great prophets of God have opposed at all times, has installed itself on the pedestal of self-aggrandizement. In the religious institutions, the word of God through His emissaries is still now and then mixed in with the insipid haze of dogmas and doctrines, but the visions of the prophets, God's warnings and guidelines are tossed to the wind.

This small book shows in condensed form the great span that underlies the works of the true prophets of God, but also the devastating effects of their being disregarded by the majority of people, who are servile to the priests and have not followed the word of God. Starting with Abraham all the way to Gabriele, the prophetess and emissary of God in our time, the one Spirit, the All-Intelligence, has been working for the one plan, which lies in the fulfillment of the prayer that Jesus, the Christ, taught – the Lord's Prayer, in which it is said: "On Earth as it is in heaven."

The Word of the Prophets of God
Is Being Fulfilled.
From Abraham to Gabriele

Most people, particularly those in so-called Christianity, consider the works of God's prophets in the history of mankind to be an event of minor significance in their everyday life or even plays no role at all. We accept the appearance of the great admonishers and proclaimers, of the emissaries of God, as an historical event, whereby an unknown God, more or less randomly, conveys His word through human beings.

How this word comes about, where this word – the word of God – comes from, even, where this God comes from, who reveals Himself, what He is like and what the word of revelation of the Eternal One is all about vanishes in the darkness of institutional lore. Cloaked in pagan-influenced, musty interpretations by church doctrine, the sight for the content of the revealed word of God became clouded.

Even though it was also reported in the traditional Bibles how Jesus interpreted the scriptures regarding the prophets and His coming, few people are aware that His explanations refer to what takes place in the temporal and that has its origin in the spiritual and is based on God's plan.

To the disciples in Emmaus, Christ said the following:

O foolish ones, and slow of heart to believe all that the prophets have spoken! Was it not necessary that the Christ should suffer these things and enter into his glory? And beginning with Moses and all the Prophets, he interpreted to them in all the Scriptures the things concerning himself.

These words show that the works of all of God's emissaries are not some kind of patchwork quilt that developed by chance, in which the word of the Eternal is brought to the people here and there. The prophetic Spirit, which is active through the bearers of the word, is embedded in the great plan of the Kingdom of God to guide back again to the Kingdom of God the Fall-beings, which, in the very basis of their souls, are divine beings from the eternal homeland. Through the call of His messengers, the Eternal, the universal, free Spirit, God, wants to move us human beings to turn back and change our ways and to show us the way: the way home, back to the Father's house.

This is the divine-spiritual plan that, throughout all times, is behind the works of all true prophets of God, and at that, until this very day. The entire history of mankind is inseparably linked with the call of the Eternal through the bearers of His word.

Like pearls threaded on a string, the word of God is directed to us human beings according to the people's state of consciousness of the respective time and their society in an ever broader and more comprehensive scope, with ever more in-depth spiritual teachings.

One Mission, One Divine Spiritual Plan Is at the Basis of the Works of All Prophets of God

High spirit beings were, and are, incarnated in the great prophets of God, who were sent into the world with the divine mission to prepare themselves for His word, in order to prepare the return into the kingdom of the eternal Being of His children, His sons and daughters, who, in the very basis of our souls, we all are.

Jesus of Nazareth indicated this mighty plan of God in the parable of the vineyard owner, who sent his servants to the disobedient tenants, who killed them all. When nothing helped, He sent his son, but the vineyard tenants also killed him. In the parable, Jesus, the Christ, is speaking of His own history, but also of the emissaries, the so-called servants, that is, the servants of God, the bearers of His word, who are high spirit beings before the throne of God.

Today, through Gabriele, the prophetess and emissary of God in our time, we know about the tremendous spiritual-divine plan, which is at the basis of the works of all the great prophets of God. It is *one* stream, from which the bearers of God's word draw. It is *one* mission, for which they are active. It is the all-encompassing desire of the eternal Father to again draw all His creation-children to His Father-heart, into the inherent laws of the eternal Being that are the laws of life of the Kingdom of God. The will of God and His desire are conveyed solely through His emissaries.

His will is the ironclad law of infinity. Excerpts of these eternal laws – insofar as people were able to grasp them – were given at all times, through people sent by God and who receive God's blessing: His prophets – and not through those who attribute the blessing to themselves: the priests. This is why God always guided the bearers of His word out from under the spell of the priest hierarchies.

As stated: The spiritual-divine plan, the return of all fallen beings to the eternal Father's house, is at the root of the works of all true prophets of God.

The Prophetic Word of God:
Throughout Millennia – The One Source

In the following, we want to take a closer look at the string of pearls, the pearls of the prophetic word of God, which, uninterruptedly throughout the millennia, lets us recognize this great plan of God: from Abraham, about 4000 years ago, to Gabriele today.

The point is not to present an unbroken historical progression, but to present the great bow, which has been spanned for us by the bearers of the word. In all cultures and at all times, God sent His messengers to guide the people to justice and peace, to turning away from violence and cruelty.

In all cultures however, something similar took place: The bearers of God's word were persecuted, banished and often killed. The teachings, the word of the Eternal, were suppressed or twisted, partly falsified beyond recognition and woven into the prevailing cult hierarchies of priests.

Abraham: The Progenitor in Recognizing the One God

Nearly 4000 years ago, in the midst of polytheism, superstition, the cult of Baal and religions based on sacrificial cults, the Eternal revealed Himself as the One God to Abraham. Thus, Abraham is the patriarch in recognizing the One God. Through him, the Eternal called upon the people of his time to strive toward Him, the All-One, and to distance themselves from the entrenched cult doings of the priestly religions, which then, as today, led the people astray with ritual acts and ceremonies – back then, the most diverse gods and idols were supposed to be appeased. Today, the pagan follow-up model of the priestly cult of Baal, the idolatry in the entourage of today's institutional cult religions, is paid homage with this.

Through Abraham, God mightily refuted polytheism during a time in which the people followed the delusions of the priestly cult religions back then, with the concept of many gods and idols, which they wanted to appease through ritual acts and move to protect the people or to secure advantages for them.

Into this time, the Eternal spoke to Abraham and told him that he should leave his father's house and go to a land that the Eternal would show him. According to what has been passed down, the Eternal said to him: *I will make of you a great nation, and I will bless you.*

Here, God's plan is seen for the first time, to build a people that is to inhabit a land in which God's blessing is active, because the people live united in His Spirit. The Eternal guided Abraham away from the metropolis of Ur back then and promised him a land in which Abraham and His own would be blessed. Trustingly, Abraham left his ancestral land and set out, guided solely by God's word to him.

Abraham recognized God as the One God, as the "I Am the I Am." Over and over again, the Eternal admonished the people in the Old Covenant not to follow the illusions of priestly cult religions, but to recognize Him, the only Eternal One, the true God, who was, who is and who will always be, and to practice justice toward all that lives.

Centuries went by, some of the people accepted the one God, others cleaved to the cults. Instead of building a people to whom a land is entrusted, and that receives God's blessing, the people became dependent and enslaved under the Egyptians.

Through Moses, the Eternal Revealed
the Basis for the Life in a Promised Land:
The Ten Commandments

Once again, the call of the Eternal took hold of a person: Moses. He heard the voice of God, which said to Him that He would lead him and his people to a promised land where milk and honey flow.

But it did not stop with this promise alone. The Eternal revealed excerpts from the eternal law of the heavens, the Ten Commandments, as ethical guidelines for the life of the individual, which are the prerequisites for the development of a people in a promised land. The promise of the promised land and the fulfillment of the Ten Commandments are mutually dependent.

They are often considered separate from each other: here a land that bestows blessing, and there the commandments of God. This way of thinking has its source in the priestly cult of miracles, which replaces the inherent laws that are lived with a covenant of mysteries.

From God, the Eternal, Moses received the Ten Commandments, which again brought the One God home to the people – the first commandment says: *I am the Lord, your God. You shall have no gods before me.*

Through His prophets, the Eternal wanted to lead the people into the promised land. For this, through Moses, He gave them the Ten Commandments, expressed in simple words, as the rules of life for every person who wants to honor the One God in his life.

The Adversary of the Emissaries of God: The Cult Priesthood

Aaron, however, the elder brother of Moses, turned away from the clear commandments of the one God. He established a cult priesthood again and created a cult religion, which put the priesthood with its cult of idols over the word of the Eternal; significantly, he himself became the first high priest of his cult religion. Meanwhile, not even the church institutions deny anymore that Moses did not write the so-called "five books of Moses," at all. Much of what is contained in the so-called books of Moses was wrongly attributed to God's prophet. A great deal is in crass contradiction to what the Eternal taught in the Ten Commandments through Moses.

The all-encompassing commandment that leads to unity *You shall not kill* was ignored in favor of priestly ritual acts and twisted into its opposite, when the priests of the new cult, the Aaron cult, were ordered to sacrifice animals to the priestly cult, that is, to sacrifice the creation-children of the All-One on the altar, which turned into an animal slaughter bank.

Moses, the prophet of God, certainly remained faithful to the commandments of his God, who clearly commanded: *You shall not kill.* However, in the name of Moses, the priesthood laid down ritual laws that were to bring about the downfall of this central commandment. The God of life, who through Moses brought the commandment *You shall not kill*, now supposedly found pleasure in having the blood of His creation-children splattered on the altars, in having the fat of unblemished lambs and calves sacrificed to Him, allegedly *as a pleasing aroma to the Lord*, as it says. He, the Eternal, who indeed commanded through Moses: *You shall not kill* is supposed to have commanded murder and lynching, robbing and plundering.

Many people did not listen to God's word through His prophet. They rejected the commandments of God and instead obeyed the numerous laws of the priests, which did constrain them, but allowed them more leeway for a depraved lifestyle in terms of ethics and morals.

Priestly cult instead of knowledge of God, vices instead of higher ethics, animal sacrifices on external altars instead of sacrificing sinfulness on the inner alter became prevalent. God's call through Moses faded away for the most part and became overrun with priestly rituals and legal regulations: Instead of God's commandments – priestly laws and forbiddances through the caste of priests.

Years, decades, centuries passed. Through the fulfillment of the commandments of God, people could have found their way to freedom and to peace. But once more, they attached themselves to cults that enabled them to continue practicing their customs, acquired at the fleshpots of Egypt.

*Once Again, a High Spirit Being Came
From the Kingdom of God and Became
a Human Being in Order to Serve God,
the Eternal, as Prophet: Isaiah*

The pearls of the word of God reached the people over and over again through the Eternal's emissaries, that is, also after Moses. High spirit beings came anew from the Kingdom of God and became human beings, to announce as prophets the law of freedom, unity and justice: thus, also the Cherub of divine Wisdom, who was active in Isaiah.

Through him, the great prophet of God, the Eternal spoke mightily to the people of Isaiah's time. They are words that continue to hold true into the present time. He called on the people to practice justice instead of idolatry, to cultivate empathy and helpfulness instead of sacrificial carryings-on.

The Eternal again spoke through Isaiah that He is the All-One who does not dwell in temples of stone.

Is there a God besides Me? There is no Rock; I know not any. And ... what is the house which you would build for me ... All these things my hand has made.

With these words through Isaiah that have been passed down, the Eternal refers to His omnipresence. Today, with this central message from God, the circle closes.

All these things my hand has made; there is no other God besides me. In these short phrases, what is passed down is that, already through Isaiah, God, the Eternal, revealed Himself as the Creator-power of the All-Unity, just as in a comprehensive way today through Gabriele, we are given an understanding of God as the speaking All-Unity.

*Through Isaiah, the Eternal
Raised His Voice Mightily
Against Animal Sacrifice and Idolatry*

Because God's hand has "made all these things," He pilloried animal sacrifice in clear words through Isaiah – He said:

What to me is the multitude of your sacrifices? says the LORD; I have had enough of burnt offerings of rams and the fat of well-fed beasts; I do not delight in the blood of bulls, or of lambs, or of goats. When you come to appear before me, who has required of you this trampling of my courts?

Bring no more vain offerings; incense is an abomination to me. New moon and Sabbath and the calling of convocations – I cannot endure iniquity and solemn assembly. Your new moons and your appointed feasts my soul hates; they have become a burden to me; I am weary of bearing them.

When you spread out your hands, I will hide my eyes from you; even though you make many prayers, I will not listen; your hands are full of blood. Wash yourselves; make yourselves clean; remove the evil of your deeds from before my eyes; cease to do evil, learn to do good; seek justice, correct oppression; bring justice to the fatherless, plead the widow's cause!

Thus spoke the One God, the God of eternity, the Father of all life, through Isaiah with mighty words, in order to move the people to turn back and change their ways.

Through the bearer of the word, Isaiah, the Eternal also decisively opposed idolatry, which, after Abraham, and despite the commandments of God through Moses, had again spread:

Their land is filled with idols; they bow down to the work of their hands, to what their own fingers have made.

The denouncement through Isaiah was connected with the prophetic admonishment:

And the idols shall utterly pass away. And people shall enter the caves of the rocks and the holes of the ground, from before the terror of the Lord, and from the splendor of his majesty, when he rises to terrify the earth. In that day mankind will cast away their idols of silver and their idols of gold, which they made for themselves to worship, to the moles and to the bats, to enter the caverns of the rocks and the clefts of the cliffs, from before the terror of the Lord, and from the splendor of his majesty, when he rises to terrify the earth.

And further:
All who fashion idols are nothing, and the things they delight in do not profit ... Who fashions a god or casts an idol that is profitable for nothing? Behold, all his companions shall be put to shame, and the craftsmen are only human. Let them all assemble, let them stand forth. They shall be terrified; they shall be put to shame together.

With vivid words, the absurdity of idolatry, of the worship of figures, is pilloried:

The ironsmith takes a cutting tool and works it over the coals. He fashions it with hammers and works it with his strong arm. ...

The carpenter stretches a line; he marks it out with a pencil. He shapes it with planes and marks it with a compass. He shapes it into the figure of a man, with the beauty of a man, to dwell in a house. He cuts down cedars, or he chooses a cypress tree or an oak and lets it grow strong among the trees of the forest. He plants a cedar and the rain nourishes it. Then it becomes fuel for a man. He takes a part of it and warms himself; he kindles a fire and bakes bread. Also he makes a god and worships it; he makes it an idol and falls down before it. Half of it he burns in the fire. Over the half he eats meat; he roasts it and is satisfied. Also he warms himself and says, Aha, I am warm, I have seen the fire! And the rest of it he makes into a god, his idol, and falls down to it and worships it. He prays to it and says, Deliver me, for you are my god!

They know not, nor do they discern, for he has shut their eyes, so that they cannot see, and their hearts, so that they cannot understand. No one considers, nor is there knowledge or discernment to say, Half of it I burned in the fire; I also baked bread on its coals; I roasted meat and have eaten. And shall I make the rest of it an abomination? Shall I fall down before a block of wood? He feeds on ashes; a deluded heart has led him astray, and he cannot deliver himself or say, Is there not a lie in my right hand?

Then as today: idolatry cult. Idolatry cult and veneration of saints – where is the difference here?

Isaiah Announced the Coming of the Messiah and the Kingdom of Peace

But Isaiah was not only an admonisher against priestly idolatry and their lust for murdering animals. He announced the coming of the Messiah, of the Redeemer, which was fulfilled through Jesus of Nazareth and His sacrificial deed on Golgotha.

God's promise through Isaiah, the coming of the Christ of God, has been fulfilled. God's plan, announced through His heavenly prince, the Cherub of divine Wisdom, who was active in Isaiah, has been carried out in the life and works of the Nazarene. Jesus Himself explained to His disciples the scripture of the old prophets concerning His coming.

The church institutions also believe that God, the Eternal, spoke truly through Isaiah here. Can He then have erred in the further plan? Because He announced more through Isaiah: The emergence of the Kingdom of Peace, in which creation finds its way to unity, to peace. Should this not be fulfilled? Is it merely a nice utopia? No – just as the coming of the Son of God in Jesus of Nazareth became reality, so will the emergence of the Kingdom of Peace become reality on this Earth, just as it has been promised.

Isaiah spoke:
The wolf shall dwell with the lamb, and the leopard shall lie down with the young goat, and the calf and the lion and the fattened calf together; and a little child shall lead them.
The cow and the bear shall graze; their young shall lie down together; and the lion shall eat straw like the ox.
The nursing child shall play over the hole of the cobra, and the weaned child shall put his hand on the adder's den.
They shall not hurt or destroy in all my holy mountain; for the earth shall be full of the knowledge of the Lord as the waters cover the sea.
Thus, the words of Isaiah.

The Masses' Servility to the Priests and Their Ignorance Regarding the Prophets of God

With the words of the true prophets of God, mankind at that time could have fulfilled the commandments of the Eternal. Through the application of the Sermon on the Mount of Jesus of Nazareth in everyday life, the foundation for the Kingdom of Peace of Jesus Christ could have been laid. But the majority of people remained obtuse, servile to priests and cleaving to sacrificial rituals. In the temple at Jerusalem, they sacrificed the animals, the doves, the sheep, the kid and turned the altars into death-bringing sacrificial stones, on which rivers of blood flowed.

What it was like in the temple at Jerusalem during the time of Jesus is described by Gil Yaron in Spiegel History, No. 6, 2011 (p.59): *The priests accepted only unblemished animals for sacrifice; they bound them tightly and ritually slaughtered them. The blood was caught in a golden vessel, the Masrek. In some cases, special skill was necessary: The throat of a poultry offering was slit open with the thumb nail. As the seat of the soul, blood was the most important part of the offerings. It was poured on the corners of the altar. Around the altar were "many openings for water, ... so that all the blood of the sacrifices which is collected in great quantities is washed away in the twinkling of an eye," as it says in the Letter of Aristeas, which was written by an Egyptian Jew. After the bloodshed, the intestines and the fat were burned on the altar and the rest of the animal was eaten by the priests or by the one making the offering.*

The sacrificial cult took place according to strict regulations, the offerings were precisely regulated. Prosperous people brought a goat, a cow or a sheep to the slaughter bank, the poor brought turtledoves or pigeons. A priest who sinned had to offer up an ox, a normal believer could make good on the same sin with a domestic goat.

There were also offerings that were made purely out of gratitude continues the report in Spiegel: *An animal's first litter was dedicated to the priests. Twice daily, a cow was very officially sacrificed in the name and at the expense of Caesar and of the Roman people ... Beyond that, priests offered up the permanent sacrifice, for which the Levites got the crowd in the mood with song and trumpets and signaled the people when to bow.*

The greatest prophet of all time, Jesus of Nazareth, the Son of God, stepped into this cult center, into the temple in Jerusalem, to inform the people about their disastrous goings-on and to drive the animal mongers and the money changers out of the temple. He said: *Is it not written: My house shall be called a house of prayer for all the nations. But you have made it a den of robbers.*

That is the desire of the Eternal, who wants to call His children together, in order to lead the people of all nations together into the worship of the One God, who demands no offerings of His creation-children, but instead, through His true prophets, challenges the people to sacrifice their egocentric, all-too-human carry-ings-on, which lead to discord, hatred, envy, fighting and war.

The mighty caste of priests did not tolerate this. They incited the people against Jesus and had Him nailed to the cross by the Romans. With the crucifixion, the adversary of God attempted to bring about the downfall of the Son of God, the Co-Regent of infinity and to mock Him.

The concept of the cult of blood and sacrifice continues to work into our time. In the alleged transformation of blood and flesh and by sup-posedly partaking of parts of His body, the present-day institutions cultivate the ritual of a surrogate offering, which an avenging God requires in order to forgive His creatures.

How can one mock God more than by twisting His commandments? Through the cult of priests, the lowest was raised to the highest and the highest – His law – was distorted into the lowest.

The commandment *You shall not kill* was deformed into a diabolical cult, in which it is said: *You shall kill in my honor, as a pleasing aroma to the Lord,* as it says. The sacrificial cult, with its killing rituals on the altars of the magic priests, serves solely the god of the underworld. Until today, Jesus as the sacrificial lamb is offered up to this god of the underworld in rituals of blood and flesh.

Which god wants His work of creation, right up to His firstborn, to be sacrificed, in order to be pacified? The God of the prophets does not want this – it is the will of the god of the underworld and his entourage.

But their seeming triumph over the Son of God could not conquer the free Spirit of which Jesus of Nazareth taught and which He Himself embodied. As Redeemer, His Spirit is effective in every person and in every soul, and, as the Christ of God, He continues to work in the mighty plan of redemption.

The light that He brought into the world could not be extinguished by the priest hierarchies. At all times, people gathered round the free Spirit, the God of Abraham, Isaac and Jacob, the God of Jesus of Nazareth, whom He simply called Father. It is the God of all true prophets of God. Over and over again, followers came together who strove to live according to the commandments of God. They accepted the word of truth and justice, in order to put it into practice in their life – and at that, in the meaning of the free Spirit, that is, without dogmas, cults, ceremonies and priests.

The free following in the fulfillment of God's word does not bind any person or any soul, but it signifies a danger for the maintenance of power of the respectively established priestly religions. In each case, the cult-entrenched priesthood respectively persecuted, destroyed and prevented nascent Original Christianity, the lived concept of unity of the people who wanted to give honor to God, the One.

The Abuse of the Word "Christian" by the Roman Emperor God Pontifex Maximus

Thus, even after the Redeemer-deed of Jesus, cult religions, priestly religions developed, in turn, marked by the many facets of human ideas and opinions. Paganism cast the dice for the garment of Christ, in order to wrap it around itself centuries later, at that, in the form of the Pontifex Maximus of the Roman emperor god, risen again in the papacy.

The institutions take the word "Christian" and with it envelop the cult mindset that stems from paganism. The words of the prophets of God are draped into the jumble of dogmas and belief systems and laid out as soul bait, in order to keep the spiritually impoverished and spiritually starved entourage caught in the network of the institutions. The nations are led by the tasseled thongs of the priestly religions, with the mighty hoping that religious manipulation will make the people obedient also in political proceedings, so that, like lemmings, following the spirit of the times, they slide into the pitfall. But the word of the Eternal endures, throughout all time.

The Priestly Religions Have Yet to Provide Evidence

How serious the leaders of the so-called Christian religions in state and church are about the word of the true prophets of God can be seen in the state of this world, particularly in the relationship of man to creation, to the animals, plants and the mineral kingdoms. For, where is the proof that the priestly religions will let the word of God's prophet Isaiah, the great vision of the Kingdom of Peace of Jesus Christ on Earth, become reality? Where is even an attempt, a beginning, in wanting to give evidence that man can again be guided into unity with nature, with its plants and animals?

There is none – the opposite is the case: Against the promise of Isaiah, against the vision of the Kingdom of Peace of Jesus Christ, the external religions adhere to discord and separation, not only toward people who believe differently, but also in the isolation and suppression of all other life forms that do not have a human face, which on many has already become an ego-distorted mask.

Instead of evidence, the institutional churches have brought the opposite, by banning as utopia the Kingdom of Peace, the actualization of the Sermon on the Mount, into another world.

But then we have to wonder:
Why institutional religions at all, if they misappropriate the fulfillment of the core tenets of the great prophets, whose names they invoke themselves, by denigrating it as a utopia for another world? To what end, the many billions in state subsidies – for a religion that degrades the prophets of God as visionaries for another world?
To what end, state subsidies of billions – for external religions that treat the teachings of Jesus of Nazareth, in whose name they let themselves be paid, like an illusion that cannot

be lived in this world, projecting them into another world? Is God a fantasist?

Is God a utopian, when, through His emissaries, He announced, and announces, the Kingdom of Peace? What a waste of energy and what an impertinence at the expense of His human children would God have allowed Himself here through His prophets? What deceit by God would it be if He were to demand that people fulfill a teaching that cannot be fulfilled at all on this Earth?

This is institutional church thinking and attributes fantasy to the great Spirit of life. Jesus, the Christ, is degraded into a utopian, who allegedly fought, lived and died for a teaching that supposedly cannot be fulfilled at all by people on this side of life.

Jesus Himself spoke to the ignorant Pharisees of His time:
Why do you not understand what I say? It is because you cannot bear to hear my word. You

are of your father the devil, and your will is to do your father's desires. He was a murderer from the beginning, and does not stand in the truth, because there is no truth in him. When he lies, he speaks out of his own character, for he is a liar and the father of lies. But because I tell the truth, you do not believe me.

If the institutional churches had mustered the evidence that to them the prophetic word of the Eternal is the leading and guiding line for their actions, then now, 2700 years after Isaiah and Hosea, 2600 years after Jeremiah, 2000 years after Jesus of Nazareth, the Christ of God, the Earth would have to be a totally different place. Peace among people, peace among nations and peoples would be a matter of course. The weapons would have been reworked into plowshares. Man would live in unity with the plants and animals, yes, with the entire Mother Earth. The Earth, this wonderful dwelling planet, the jewel on the firmament of the Eternal, would flourish in the beauty of the unity that radiates out into the cosmos, the All, and it would be able to receive and absorb from the All the positive forces, the radiation and vibration of the eternal Being.

The Fruits of Priestly Deception

But what is the condition of the Earth? – 2700 years after Isaiah, 2000 years after Jesus?
It's at the edge of the abyss – and that, at the hands of man. Exhausted, poisoned and de-formed, it carries the load that man has inflicted upon it. But for how long yet?
Armed to the teeth with weapon arsenals, the mighty of this world do talk about peace, but they are ready at any time to use lethal machinery against their neighbor when it's all about preserving their status quo.

The mockery of the Christ of God takes place especially in those countries where the rulers invoke Jesus, the Prince of Peace, who said: *All who take the sword will perish by the sword.* Billions are available for the war machinery; in comparison, for the relief of hardship, it is an alibi amount. Tens of thousands of people starve to death every day, because artificially bred animals are fattened with the bulging sacks of grain of the sated ones. Especially those nations that have put themselves under the yoke of the institutional churches and have also put their stamp on other nations are responsible for the impending disaster, which is downplayed, and called "climate change." People's imperiousness and lust for power have brought this Earth to the edge of the abyss.

The conjurers of idols may very well use the words of the Eternal in their speeches, but it is merely lip service that they mix and bend with their lore and human concepts, to thus make these serve the exploitative egomania of mankind.

Once again the question: Which religion has so far given evidence that their God is the God who leads to justice and peace? A glance into this world shows that the evidence has failed to materialize. Instead of the good fruits of justice, which stem from the awareness of the unity of all Being, one sees the fruits of priestly deception and of all those who let, and still let, themselves be deceived by this.

But the word of God is valid: *For truly I tell you: Until heaven and earth pass away, not one iota nor the least stroke will disappear from the law, until everything is accomplished.* Note well: His word – not the word of priests.

God, the Eternal, said: *The earth is mine.* The Earth will remain His. But it will be cleansed of the deposits of human egoism, of the brutality, which led to poisoning, destruction and devastation. Mankind will have to bear the consequences of its actions, which emerged from the satanic desire of wanting to rob the Eternal of what is His: creation, the Earth with its minerals, plants and animals. Again and again, the Eternal called the people to turn back and change their ways, but the human ear remained deaf.

In order to silence and suppress the fear of the consequences of their own actions, the majority of people turned to incense-clouded, stupefying rituals, with indulgences and confession-rituals, which do not remedy the causes, but encourage further offences.

Priestly Masters of Ceremonies
Pay Homage to Their Self-made Idols

No prophet ever founded an external religion, through which people are tied to rituals, dogmas and doctrinal systems. Through no prophet did the free Spirit, who is the unity of all life, appoint intercessors, via whom the communication with His creation-children should take place.

Why did Jesus of Nazareth teach us in the Lord's Prayer the direct communication with God, whom we may address as Father, and why do the churches teach the opposite of this, by shoving the priests as intercessors between God and His child?

In His mighty word of revelation, the Eternal directly led, and leads, people into taking responsibility for their own feeling, thinking and acting, but also for all that lives. But the priestly religions installed themselves, in order to bind the people to themselves and their cults. They built stone houses and placed idols in them, to whose idolotrous images they and their hangers-on, the people, should pray. Right up until this very day, people kneel before so-called saints, even though at all times, the word of the true prophets of God pilloried idolatry. To this, more words of God through Isaiah: *When you cry out, let your collection of idols deliver you! The wind will carry them all off, a breath will take them away. But he who takes refuge in me shall possess the land and shall inherit my holy mountain.*

In the priestly religions back then as today, the masters of ceremonies pay homage to their self-made images of idols. They call upon God with their harping speeches, in which they invoke mysteries and let themselves be paid a lot for their mystery-shrouded God and his idolatry by the people, above whom they deliberately elevate themselves with elaborate garments. They seek to expand and enhance their sinecures. Their pasture is the people, which, willing to pay, accepts the ritual acts without question along with their occult priests and without examining their truth in the light of the true prophets of God.

The institutions brazenly claim that the prophetic office has been transferred to the priests, saying that when a priest or bishop speaks in his teaching capacity, then God speaks through him.

However, we can read in the books of Moses, on which the institutions base themselves:

And if you say in your heart, "How may we know the word that the Lord has not spoken?" – when a prophet speaks in the name of the LORD, if the word does not come to pass or come true, that is a word that the Lord has not spoken; the prophet has spoken it presumptuously. You need not be afraid of him.

The works of the priestly religions themselves have supplied evidence for what they have aligned themselves to. For no religion has given evidence of the truth of God's word by fulfilling what was announced through the prophets: to guide the life of the Earth with its minerals, plants, animals and human beings into unity, in which each living being finds its worthy place as a creation-child of God. Evidence has not been given by the external religions that they let God's word come alive and that they stand in the fulfillment of the promise of God's prophets, so that they, as the Eternal said through

Isaiah: *shall possess the land and shall inherit my holy mountain,* the land that is *full of the knowledge of the Lord as the waters cover the sea.*

Not only Isaiah, but also Hosea, Jeremiah and Jesus as well as many other bearers of God's word announced the Kingdom of Peace, and also the fulfillment of a covenant with God, which would become manifest in the unity of all life between man, nature and animals. If the religions had fulfilled the promises of God's prophets, they would have proven the truth of God's word, and the Earth would be in a different state today.

The Eternal Announced a Covenant with the Animals – The Institutional Churches Keep Sacrificing His Creatures

Through the prophet Hosea, the Eternal announced the making of a covenant with the animals of the forests, the fields, yes, with the whole Earth. But the church institutions deny that animals have a soul. They view them as beings without a spirit that are controlled only by instinct. So with what is the Eternal supposed to make a covenant? With soulless carcasses?

Only someone who has turned, not to say, deformed, his body into a sacrificial altar for the meat of carcasses cannot comprehend the soul in the animals with their fine sensations, with their traits that are filled with character and life. His feelings toward creation are dulled.

For centuries, the institutions of the so-called Christian churches have been contradicting the word of God that was given through prophets. They have crowned themselves as the crown of creation, whose sacrifice on their self-made altars is creation. The state of this Earth clearly shows where this has led.

Many generations have heard His word and tossed it to the wind. Through envy, hatred, animosity, hostilities that include belligerent actions, man against man, nation against nation, man against nature and against the animals, many people have spoiled for themselves the possibility of creating the basis for a life in the awareness of the unity and the freedom of the great All-One.
Unspeakable suffering was caused to people, but also to all of nature on the Earth, because the prophetic Spirit, the call of the Eternal, was at all times tossed to the wind by the majority of people.

The lawful plan of redemption, which went forth from the Kingdom of God, was, and is, constantly torpedoed by the opposing forces that belong to the adversary of God. Not only are the bearers of God's word attacked and persecuted through the respective ruling caste of priests and, depending on the prevailing spirit of the time and the circumstances connected with it, are silenced through murder or character assassination, but the word itself – where it couldn't be repressed – was also appropriated by the cult priests and, when possible, falsified and used wrongly. Around the word of God through the prophets, they draped their priestly words which, in part hardly noticeably, but consistently, perverted the statements of God's prophets into their opposite.

This becomes most clearly visible in Moses. God's commandment through Moses reads: *You shall not kill.* In the so-called books of Moses, however, which are largely priestly scriptures, murder and manslaughter were allegedly ordered by God. The fight of the caste of priests against God's prophets is also clearly recognizable with Moses and Aaron. Aaron introduced the Golden Calf while Moses received the law of God. Aaron established the priestly cult. Later, much of this was attributed to Moses.

In his book "Prophetic Thinkers. Do Not Extinguish the Spirit!" Walter Nigg, a Lutheran theologian and church historian, describes priests as the natural enemy of the prophet. And so, since God speaks through His true prophets, but the priest is the natural enemy of the prophets, then whom does the priest serve? It was priests colored by the times who placed Jesus on the cross. It was the priests who had Stephen stoned by the Romans. It was always the cult priests who acted against the word of God. Why? Because through His true prophets, God always exposed the priesthood, just as Jesus also spoke to the people of that time: ... *but you are not to be called rabbi.* Translated into the present time, this is: You are not to be called pastor, priest, bishop or pope, for you are all brothers and sisters. Only One is your teacher, Christ.

The priests, who pretend to be intercessors for God, have made of God a product whose label they cling to and for which they have symbolically applied for a patent. Anyone who wants to find God without them is taken to court. He is excluded from salvation, eternally. Their claim, "Without us, no contact with God," is, measured against the words of Jesus, pure blasphemy, pure profanity. It is the core of the satanic thought of wanting to be greater than God and of separating God from His creation. The "divide, bind and rule" is the creed of the priestly cult-religions, no matter of what color. On the other hand, the word of God's prophets is under the seal of God: "Link and be."

Priestly religions have been established for their own benefit and for the benefit of the mighty. In differing ways, they bled and bleed the people, who submissively follow them, in order to allegedly be represented by them before the law of God.

The cult religions have spread over this Earth like an octopus, in order to suck dry the nations and place them in their service.

As Jesus of Nazareth, Christ said that He did not come to abolish the law of the prophets but to fulfill it. He spoke of fulfillment, not of cults, tradition, dogmas and rituals, and He gave us a criterion by which we can recognize the works in His Spirit. The criterion is: *You shall know them by their fruits.* This means that the deed in His Spirit bears good fruit. Where bad fruits appear, it is not Him who is at work there, but His adversary.

You Shall Know Them by Their Fruits

Why, after 2000 years, in which church institutions refer to Him and worldwide have become the greatest cult religion of mankind, is the world at the edge of the abyss? The simple criterion, put into our hand by Jesus, sheds light on this: *You shall know them by their fruits.* Today the bad seed is sprouting; the harvest of the bad fruit is underway.

Why? Because no religion has given evidence that it wants the Kingdom of Peace announced by God's prophets to become reality.

Where does so-called Christianity stand? Where do the mighty, influential institutions of the cult priests stand with their billions upon billions that they have stripped from the people over the centuries? Are they in the fulfillment of the Sermon on the Mount, so that one could say: By their good fruits, we can recognize that they are active in His Spirit, in the Spirit of the Christ of God?

Quite to the contrary. Intrigues, hierarchical wrangling, pomposity, greed for power, even to child abuse and its cover-up, these are the cult-embellished excesses on the family tree of the priestly religions.

In many cases, these are the bad fruits of a cult, whose pinnacle of mockery consists of the fact that it invokes Jesus, the Christ – Him, who back then, castigated the cult priests with sharp words: *For you are like whitewashed tombs, which outwardly appear beautiful, but within are full of dead people's bones and all uncleanness.*

The Care of the Soul Cannot Be Delegated

Many people have blindfolds put on them by the blind leaders of the blind, in the delusion that they could transfer the development of their soul's salvation to a priest.

The responsibility of the individual was handed over to priests, even though God, the Eternal, always spoke directly to the people through His emissaries – and not by way of priests. Every individual is asked to bear responsibility for the word of the Eternal, which He directed to all of mankind.

Anyone who lets himself by bound by representatives – whether they call themselves pastor, priest, bishop or even pope – anyone who has handed over his spiritual life to the professional association of ritual dealers in indulgences, the priests, is in danger of crossing the threshold of death into the beyond without a living, activated consciousness. His perhaps pitifully developed soul will find itself again, or still, bound to the world of concepts of the priesthood, until it recognizes that the care and unfolding of the soul cannot be delegated to another person, to no priest, no pastor, no bishop, no pope.

In the Sermon on the Mount, Jesus of Nazareth addressed each and every individual. He did not convene a flock of priests and conduct a council to issue dogmas. He called upon the people to follow Him, of their own free will, and not by way of a baptism of the underaged, not through intercessors, not through the hierarchies of the cult-priesthood.

Each and every individual is called upon, when it is about establishing the Kingdom of Peace on this Earth through the fulfillment of the divine-spiritual laws, as they were conveyed by God's emissaries, His prophets, and in particular, by Jesus, the Christ.

His Word Through the Emissary of God – Gabriele

Before He became the Redeemer of all souls and men on Golgotha, He announced His coming in the Spirit, as the ruler of the Kingdom of Peace. He announced the Comforter, the Spirit of Truth, who will lead us into all the truth. What He promised, He has kept. Ever more prolifically, the Eternal has passed on the fullness of His eternal word to the people. The Eternal's mighty plan of redemption lies at the root of the word of all true prophets of God, which, in retrospect, rolls out like a string of pearls. Ever more mightily, in ever deeper and more comprehensive revelations, He spoke, and speaks, through His messengers. Anyone who is able to comprehend the words of God's true prophets sees therein the Wisdom of God, which runs like a shining thread through all the revelations given through His emissaries.

From Abraham and through the prophets of the Old Covenant all the way to Jesus, the Christ, His word, the truth of the heavens, flowed in an ever mightier stream to us human beings. Inexhaustible as eternity itself, through His instruments, the Eternal pours His word out of His horn of plenty among the people, insofar as they can grasp it.

For over 36 years, the Eternal has now been speaking to us in a mighty stream, through His prophetess and messenger, the emissary of God, Gabriele. In an unprecedented scope and in all details, He teaches us the inherent laws of the eternal Being, insofar as they can be passed on using the means of expression of the human language in three dimensions.

Through Gabriele, He taught, and teaches, us all that His disciples could not yet bear at that time. Through her, He completes His teaching activity, the work of enlightenment and guidance to God in us, who dwells in the very basis of every person.

The comprehensive word of eternity, insofar as it can be passed on in the insufficient language of three dimensions, that is, in our human language, was, and is being, transmitted into all four winds through television stations and radio stations. Untiringly, He calls to His own to become aware of their divine-spiritual origin, of the filiation of God, which wants to again guide together all people as His sons and daughters.

The All-Being, God, the Eternal, is unchangeable. He speaks in the I AM THE I AM, from eternity to eternity. His message is the message from the eternal homeland to all His human children. What He calls into the world through His prophets holds true yesterday, today and tomorrow. It will remain in the Earth's atmosphere, until it is fulfilled through those who follow His word, by fulfilling in their life, step by step, the inherent laws of the eternal Being.

God's word through Gabriele is carried out into the whole world in an indescribable fullness. At the beginning, Gabriele traveled to many countries of this Earth, and God, the Eternal, and Christ, the Son of God, gave mighty revelations before countless people. At times, there were audiences of over 1000 people who listened to the word of God and could experience how the spiritual world spoke through Gabriele, frequently for more than an hour.

For people who could not experience this unique event themselves, it is somewhat inconceivable, as was expressed by a young man visiting the Sophia library. Just like many people worldwide, he is familiar with the messages from the All through television programs and CDs. Totally interested, he then asked: "Tell me, were you there at a revelation? Was it really *live*? Was there no paper, no manuscript?" Many people can bear witness to this: Yes, it was and is God, the Eternal, who often spoke, and speaks, for over an hour, freely from within; it is the word of God, the word of the Creator of the All.

This mighty event truly is nearly incomprehensible. Because for a prophet of God it takes the utmost concentration to hear the word of God in his innermost being, so as to pass it on in his mother tongue, not letting himself be diverted by anything in the process. Never before in the history of mankind has there been greater testimony for the prophetic Spirit as in the revealed word of God through Gabriele before so many thousands of people worldwide.

The unadulterated word of God has been given. It can be freely examined by every person. The *Sophia Library* contains the great treasure of God's unadulterated word; it is the Ark of the Covenant of the free Spirit. The unadulterated word of God has been translated into many languages and is freely accessible to every person.

Through Isaiah, the Eternal announced that He would raise a banner, which for a second time would gather His own from all four winds. The banner has been raised; the Spirit of the Christ of God speaks to us people. For over 36 years, as stated, the word of the Eternal and of His Son, the Co-Regent of eternity, Christ, has been going out into all four winds through His emissary, Gabriele. He gathers His own, who let themselves be touched by His Spirit and prepare themselves to again establish together what is announced in the vision of Isaiah: the Kingdom of Peace, in which nothing bad is done anymore "in all His holy mountain."

Through the prophet Hosea, the Eternal announced, as stated, a covenant with the animals. He said:

And I will make for them a covenant on that day with the beasts of the field, the birds of the heavens, and the creeping things of the ground. And ... I will make you lie down in safety.

That day is here. During our time, a further part of His divine plan is being fulfilled.

The Eternal is carrying out what He announced to mankind through His prophets:

The foundation of the Kingdom of Peace of Jesus, the Christ, is being established during this time. Through His emissary, Gabriele, whom God, the Eternal, calls His prophetess and emissary, the cornerstone has been laid, in order to implement His word, given through Isaiah, Hosea and other prophets, through the work of the deed of love for neighbor, toward people, nature and animals.

From this emerged – and it continues to develop – the proof of the truth of the teachings of the Eternal, who is the one God: the God of Abraham, the God of Moses and Isaiah, the God of Jesus of Nazareth and of all true prophets. The foundation stone has been laid. The cornerstone, which the religious institutions have discarded, will become the coping stone. God's plan is being fulfilled. In their comprehensive meaning, the fragments of the passed-down words through the great prophets of God are only becoming visible again through the unadulterated word of God in our time.

Thanks to Gabriele, we now understand the words of the Eternal that were passed down to us through Isaiah:
Heaven is my throne, and the earth is my footstool; what is the house that you would build for me, ...? All these things my hand has made...

It is the speaking All-Unity, the All-life, that speaks to us and wants to guide us to the awareness of the unity of all Being. With their theological constructs and splendid buildings, the religions have split mankind. Mutual ostracism, up to wars embellished by religion, were, and are, the consequences.

At all times, the speaking God of the true prophets of God sent His messengers to lead people out of their priestly delusion. The prophetic Spirit is always the Spirit of freedom and justice, the Spirit of the unity of all Being. Wherever anything else is encountered, it is not from God.

Through God's word-bearers from Abraham to Gabriele, the spiritual bow was spanned; the divine plan is revealed.
The Cherub of divine Wisdom, once in the earthly garment as God's great prophet Isaiah, is responsible for the Kingdom of Peace of Jesus Christ on Earth. His spirit-dual is incarnated in Gabriele. In unity, they work for the plan of God. The cradle of creation was saved by the Redeemer-deed of the Christ of God. His light

radiates in every soul and in every person. The awareness of the communality of all Being, as it is taught today through Gabriele, leads people step by step toward again opening their origin in themselves, the divine Self, the divine Being, which is inherent in the core of being of every person. From developing the awareness that each person is a son or a daughter of God and that our fellow creatures are also from the breath of God, opens up a totally different way of dealing with nature, with the plants, with the minerals and the animals. People will learn to recognize the animals as their little brothers and sisters. They will perceive in the plants developing beings, which, like them, are from the All-Unity of God. The minerals will no longer be treated carelessly, so that man, nature and animals again find their way to the unity that they are, since eternity, from the Creator-Spirit of the All – beings from His origin, from the power of the Creator-God.

On Earth as It Is in Heaven –
The Concept of Unity
for a New Humanity

In this awareness, Gabriele founded the International Gabriele Foundation, which today radiates out worldwide as role model and guiding star for further foundations, especially in Africa. People of good will are called worldwide to help build up the concept of unity, which says: *on Earth as it is in heaven.*

From this lived concept of unity, a new humanity with higher ethics and morals is developing very gradually. It will be a humanity of freedom, a humanity of a conscious lifestyle in the respect for creation and in the knowledge of the unity of all Being.

The land announced by God's great prophets is here! It forms the basis that radiates out and builds up further oases of life, *predominantly* in Africa. Africa is the cradle of humankind, and Africa will be the cradle of a new humanity, which has accepted the higher ethics and morals of Jesus of Nazareth and is helping to build up the land for the coming of the Christ of God in Spirit.

A most intense communication already exists between the ever-expanding Land of Peace and the cradle in Africa. The child still lies in the cradle, but when it grows out of the cradle then it will mature and there will be people who live in the fulfillment of the higher ethics and morals. Then the circle to the Land of Peace of the mighty International Gabriele Foundation for the New Era is completed.

The beginning has been made; as mentioned, the child still lies in the cradle. But it will outgrow the cradle and it will be:

The Land of Peace,
the Fulfillment of the Visions of All
Great Prophets of God

To conclude this book, may a word of the Eternal be stated, given through the great prophet of God, Isaiah. It makes clear that the word of the prophets is being fulfilled.

As the rain and the snow come down from heaven, and do not return to it without watering the earth and making it bud and flourish, so that it yields seed for the sower and bread for the eater, so is my word that goes out from my mouth: it will not return to me empty, but will accomplish what I desire and achieve the purpose for which I sent it. (Isaiah 55:10-11).

Read also ...

This Is My Word

A and Ω

The Gospel of Jesus

The Christ Revelation
Which True Christians the World
Over Have Come to Know

A book that lets you know about Jesus, the Christ. The truth of His work and life as Jesus of Nazareth.

From the Contents: Childhood and Youth of Jesus – The Falsification of the Teaching of Jesus of Nazareth – Pharisees Yesterday and Today – Jesus Loved the Animals and Always Championed Them – The Sermon on the Mount – Meaning and Purpose of Life on Earth – Prerequisites for Healing the Body – Jesus Taught About Marriage – On the Nature of God – God Does Not Rage and Punish. The Law of Cause and Effect – The Teaching of "Eternal Damnation" Is a Mockery of God – On Death, Reincarnation and Life – The Coming Times and the Future of Mankind – The True Meaning of the Deed of Redemption of Christ – and much more ...

Included is a short autobiography of Gabriele, with a charcoal drawing

1104pp., Softcover, Order No. S007en, ISBN: 978-1-890841-38-6

Ask for our catalog:
Universal Spirit
P.O. Box 3549
Woodbridge, CT 06525
USA
<u>www.Universal-Spirit.org</u>
1-800-846-2691